CONSOULATION

CONSOULATION

A Musical Meditation

BRYAN SCHWARTZ

Character: Isaac Erevan, a middle-aged Jewish man who sings and sighs.
Setting: Anywhere, any time after the Third Destruction.

Consoulation: A Musical Meditation
Words, music and book by Bryan Schwartz

Cover art: *Jerusalem, Compositia 8*, oil on canvas, 2008
by Eduard Grossman

Book and cover design by Ariel Walden, Bookraft

Printed in Canada

First Edition

ISBN 978-1-7753234-0-2

www.consoulation.ca

CONTENTS

PRELUDE: SONG I

A Lullaby in Grown Up Time

(Instrumental)

SONG 2

Back Again

I can't recall the voices of this morning
Whom I met or what they had to say
They cannot seem to capture my attention
Some muffled noise and then they fade away

I can't recall at all about last week
Whom I met or what I had to say
I cannot seem to capture my attention;
Somewhere back there guess I lost my way

You'd think that after all these years
The echoes would all disappear
Instead I almost hear you say
My child it's going to be okay
And I am here with you today
I'm back again
I'm back again
I'm back again
I'm back again

I'll never been the man that I'm supposed to be
I've flailed around and failed and found it rough
Yet suddenly I almost hear you say to me
You'll always be my boy and that's enough

You'd think that after all these years
The memory would disappear

Instead I almost hear you say
My child I'm here with you today
And everything will be okay

Go back again
Go back again
Go back again
Go back again

I HEARD THAT MY FATHER had passed away.

I could not think, let alone speak, let alone sing.

My little son Michael watches me as I sit in silence.

Finally he asks "Is your father in heaven?"

Do I tell him there is no heaven?

Reality has always had a way of overpowering me.

Do I tell him yes, my father is with the angels?

My father was good at telling stories. They used to cheer me up.

The setting for one of his tales is many centuries ago.

A great rabbi is aged and worn.

He has come to the end of his days on this earth.

He lies in silence as he awaits his final moment.

The rabbi has many disciples. And they have gathered, all of them, around their master's deathbed. They join in beseeching:

> *"Master, do not leave us until you have pronounced for us your final words."*

They repeat the words of the Talmud:

> *"At the hour of death, a man does not jest, and so the words of a dying man are regarded as signed, sealed and delivered."*

But their master tells them:

> *"Leave me alone;*
> *let a weary old man die in peace."*

Still the disciples press him for his final words.
Finally, with a weary gasp, the great rabbi says slowly, slowly:

> *"Life is like a river."*

Then his head slumps and his eyes close.
The disciples rush out of the room, They know they must attend to his final rites - but first they wish to understand his parting message:

> *"Life is like a river."*

One disciple argues that it is a message of hope:

> *that our life on earth is like a river;*
> *but the life hereafter is like a boundless sea.*

One disciple suggests that the rabbi may have intended a message of despair.

we are immersed in the current,
we do not see the ultimate destination
we are helpless to change it.

And so the debate grows.
The theories multiply.
Each is contested.

At the fringe of the murmuring disciples is the youngest of them.
He cannot follow much of the frothing debate.
His gaze begins to wander.
He looks back at the room where the rabbi lies
—and he notices a slight nod of the rabbi's head. . . .

Then a twitch of the rabbi's eyelids!

The youngest disciple cries out to the whole group:

"our master lives! "

—and they all rush back to the rabbi's bedside;
and behold! —
there is within the rabbi still a flicker of life.

The disciples ask their master to explain:

"Rabbi, we treasure your legacy, but we cannot fully grasp it.
What did you mean, life is like a river?
We have voiced more interpretations than we have heads to judge them.
Before you depart you must help us to understand."

The rabbi sighs a heavy sigh, and then he whispers the words that are truly final.

"All right,

he says,

"so life isn't like a river."

And then he dies.

After my father first told me that story, and while he was still alive, I wondered many times about how life is like a river and about how it isn't like a river.

And here are some stories and songs that emerged from all the wondering.

—questions;
—possibilities;
—wishful thinking;
—wistful thinking.

And by the end I will have told you what happened when my father passed away.

The Book of Chronicles says:

"our days on earth are a shadow, and there is no abiding."

Is life like a spring river that rushes to the sea and then disappears?

SONG 3

It All Washes Out in the End

When the torrents came down
Noah took to the boat
He put the animals in
And he kept out the folks
If you'd have been there
You'd have not stayed afloat
That's all, the Bible says
That's all she wrote
The inevitable truth has been ever since then
That it all washes out in the end

I had an architect friend
He spent twenty five years
He did, down by the ocean building seaside piers,
The most durable structure that he ever built
Is under the ocean and six feet of silt
'Cause nothing survives what the hurricane sends
It all washes out in the end

You build your castles high and tall
And you think they'll weather all
Don't waste your time on such hopeless hopes
Sooner or later you'll be in the moat
Eroded, corroded and finally zeroeded
It all washes out in the end

Now the optimist says it comes out in the wash,
I'm here to tell you that's piddle and posh
Defaced, effaced and finally erased
Invaded, inundated and finally negated
Eroded, corroded and finally zeroeded
It all washes out in the end

THE TALMUD SAYS that for two and half years the sages considered this great question: is it better to be born or is it better to never even exist? They finally concluded that with all life's suffering, it is better not to be born. But as long as you are here, you must reflect on what you have done in your life, and upon what you will do in the life that remains to you.

But I imagine a new born baby is only awash in the swirling sensations of the moment.

And I imagine that when a mother sings a lullaby, the words may be wrong, the notes may be off-key, the melody may drift and quaver, the timbre of the voice may be thin or harsh, but to her child the song is always . . . perfect.

I remember . . .

I am very small, and my mother is singing . . .

SONG 4

Enough for a Lullaby

Little child
I will sing you a lullaby
You don't know the words
And neither do I
Who needs syllables
When we're together?
Laila lalai lalai lalai
Lai lai lai
Lai lai la laila

Little child
I will sing you a lullaby
We'll make up the music as we go along
Who needs notes
When we're together
Mother and child make a song
Lai lai lai
Lai lai la laila

Little child
I will sing you a lullaby
You feel the peace
And so do I
Mother and child
Silent together

That is enough for a lullaby
Lai lai lai
Lai lai la laila

MY FATHER SANG me songs too. In a deep and rounded baritone. He was born near the Black Sea, and he remembered just enough to make up words and melodies that sounded like they could be Russian. And then I grew up and I forgot he ever sang them.

Here is one of the earliest things I always remembered.

We have moved to a new city. I'm the newest and youngest kid in the class. And the only Jewish one. The rest of the kids are practicing for a choir competition. The song they are singing is called "A Room of My Own". The teacher does not invite me to join them. She has me sitting at my desk, at the back, doing some tedious arithmetic.

The lead of my pencil breaks. I guess I always push down very hard on pencils when I am writing.

I don't want to disturb the other kids by using the noisy mechanical pencil sharpener.

So I try to use my teeth instead.

I nibble quietly as I can.
But still I do make a few crackly sounds.
But I do not think they are loud enough for anyone else to hear.

When the other kids have finished practicing,
the teacher rushes to my desk,
and rips the pencil from my hand,
and slaps my wrist.

I pick up the pencil,
and look at my hand,
and I tell myself:

"Someday, with this same pencil and this same hand,
I will write my very own song
And it will
ASTOUND you."

Well, maybe I didn't actually say that to myself at the time.
Back then, I didn't think I actually could make up a song.
And I would have been too shy to sing it out loud anyway.
Still, I prefer the ending the way I told it.
It makes for a better story.

You grow older still and you look for a companion soul. My father once told me this story from the Talmud. Before a child is born, a voice from heaven says who the child is to marry. I would learn as a young man that the official announcement often does not reach us down here on Earth.

SONG 5

Captain of My Soul

If I took a brand new interest
In the latest fashion styles
Could I dress the way I always have
But would you wear a smile?

If I did not worry so much
About the things that are to be
While you live inside the moment,
Would you say we're meant to be?

Captain of my fate
Mistress of my soul
Captain of my fate
Mistress of my soul

If I did not dwell so much upon unkindnesses gone by
Would you finally apologize and say we're worth a try?

Mistress of my fate
Captain of my soul
Mistress of my fate
Captain of my soul

If I changed the way I sneeze upon encountering your cat?
If I ceased my search for God above and other stuff like that?

Captain of my soul
Mistress of my fate
Captain of my soul
Mistress of my fate

If we shared the same conception of normality itself
If one of us or both of us were only someone else
Captain of my soul
Mistress of my fate
Mistress of my soul
Captain of my fate
Master of my soul

I REMEMBER THE DAY I left that mistress of my soul. I left? Well, that's what I thought to myself at the time. She feels that she is sending me away. So I get into a bus to travel to another city. I sit down, and pick up a seventeen cent ball point pen and find a big empty margin in a newspaper. And then I do something I had never even tried before.

I compose a sonnet.

I try to follow all of Shakespeare's strict rules for writing them:

> Iambic pentameter;
> that's ten syllables to every line;
> on every second vowel lies the stress;
> fourteen lines;
> three quartets of alternating rhymes;
> a culminating couplet.

I set out to write 52 sonnets.

One sonnet each week.

Each week for a year.

Fifty two.

As I was approaching sonnet number seven or so, my father noticed I had been sad and silent for a long time. He never asked why. He just seemed to know. And he finally said "Son, you have to be resilient. Look at Joseph in the book of Genesis. His own brothers sell him into slavery. He ends up in a dungeon in Egypt. But Joseph never stops dreaming. He rises up and becomes the Prime Minister of the whole country. He reunites with his brothers and finally even his old father comes to visit him."

And I said "Good point, Dad. And the whole family stays in Egypt. And their children become slaves. But as you say, everything works out. Four hundred years after Joseph's death, his descendants finally escape. And they carry his bones back home to the promised land."

My father says, "Well don't forget, the prophet Ezekiel. He sees a field of dry bones, and he makes them live again."

Well, I tried to see things my father's way, but I couldn't. As far as I could tell at the time, I was not Ezekiel, and had no magic powers.

So I'm back to writing sonnets. I keep reading Shakespeare's sonnets – and those of his more obscure contemporaries. I read Sir Phillip Sidney, Michael Drayton, Samuel Daniel. I was the only one reading them except for some old professors who were hired when Queen Elizabeth the First still reigned.

Who was ever meant to read these crystalline cries of the heart?

Were Shakespeare's sonnets intended for his dark lady? Not likely. They are laced with insolence and insult.

His wealthy patron? No. He would not have poured his proud soul into a single golden goblet.

No, I imagine Shakespeare must have been writing for his friends.

After all, who else could truly sympathize?

As the Book of Proverbs says:

> *"A friend loveth at all times, and a brother is born for adversity."*

SONG 6

My Old Friend

Hello my old friend,
Come to talk for a while
I'm straggling home from the wars of the heart
"Wounded in action," you ask with a smile,
A transplanted psyche would help for a start

So let's sit in a boat in the sun on the lake
Recount once again our disasters of yore
You'll tell me again your most roaring mistakes
Remind me of times I've been foolish before

And pass me the reel, and I'll catch us a fish
You say with my luck I'll just stir up the sharks?
You know at the moment I desperately wish
Our ball team would blow fewer games in their park

You'll find her some day, so you say as we leave
I doubt it old friend, but we'll see, we'll see

A FRIEND OF MINE used to regale me with stories about his own romantic calamities. Like the time he was on a date in a restaurant, and tried to impress her by singing some bathetic song he had heard on the radio. I could not imagine anyone doing anything stupider or more embarrassing.

Except for me.
Here is the story I told him.

I am out with a young lady who has recently immigrated from Russia. I am trying to impress her. I try to recite to her - in the original Russian - my favourite poem from my high school Russian class. It was written by the poet Sergei Esenin. Just before he hanged himself, he slashed his wrists, and wrote in his own blood these final words:

"Goodbye my friend, goodbye;
My dear, you are in my heart;
Our predestined parting promises a future meeting.

Goodbye my friend, goodbye;
Without word, without hand;
Do not mourn and do not sadden your brow;
In this life to die is nothing new
But to live of course is nothing newer."

She says "are you trying to speak Russian or something? I can't understand any of it. It sounds like gibberish."

I pause.

Then I say, "actually, it is rare dialect of lowland gibberish. There is only one native speaker left, and I hear that he's too depressed to say anything at all."

But maybe frustration, defeat and loneliness are the basis for a wider solidarity. It's not just our personal friends who have been there; haven't we all?

SONG 7

Brotherhood of Blues

Even if your grammar is quite correct
You don't mess up
When you inflect
Even if you speak ten foreign tongues
And twenty extra dialects
When she goes away
You won't have a thing you can say
When she goes away
You'll sigh
And then you'll sing those blues
You'll find some lyrics you can use
You're gonna sing those blues
You'll sing the blues
Sing those blues

Even if you've got a lot of cash
You'll feel quite poorly when she's passed
Even if you've got some real estate
You'll have nowhere you can escape
'Cause when she goes away
You won't have a place you can stay
When she goes away
You'll sigh
And then you'll sing those blues
'Cause it's time to play your dues

You're going to sing those blues
Sing those blues
Sing those blues

Even if you think you're much too white to sing the way
A black man might
Hey, it really doesn't matter what's your hue
When she leaves, you'll sing the blues
Cause when she goes away
You'll feel your colour turn to gray
When she goes away
You'll sigh
And then you sing the blues
Join the brotherhood of lose
You're gonna sing the blues
You'll sing those blues
You'll sing those blues

Even if you're an atheist
You think that Pascal's bet was fixed
Even if you never learned to pray
You'll say My Lord in your dismay
When she goes away
You'll know the soul inside your clay
When she goes away
You'll sigh

And then you sing the blues
It's the hymn book you will use
There's nothing else to choose
It's the truest of the trues
You sing those blues
Sing those blues

I WAS STILL IN THE DESERT, still writing a sonnet every week, still suffering. Adversity, the Talmud says, can be a test of our mettle and a spur to self-improvement.

> *"Whoever rejoices in the sufferings that come upon him in this life brings salvation to the world."*

A thousand years later, the folk tradition wondered if suffering was overrated. As a Yiddish Proverb says:

> *"Pray that you may never suffer all that you can endure."*

Even the Talmud tells the story of a rabbi who took to his sickbed.

He felt deathly ill.

A friend of his, also a rabbi, came to him and asked:

> *"Are your sufferings welcome to you?"*

The sick rabbi thought about it and said:

> *"I welcome neither the suffering nor its rewards"*

His friend said;

> *"Then take my hand and rise up".*

And the friend pulled the sick rabbi up from his bed,
and he was cured.

My father told me that story, and I thought of it when I reached week 46 of my Sonnet sequence.

Sonnet 46 / Shallow Youth

Shallow youth, it thinks the height of tragedy
The most profoundest thing in all of life;
Awed, it almost yearns for the intensity
Of cruel, savage, bitter, vengeful strife.
It's true, the tempest is a mighty turn;
Rain blasts, winds howl, thunder cracks, lightning burns;
But less than that, there's flooded out worms,
Soggy down -blown leaves and dead baby birds.
To know that all must die and still to live;
To understand what's been and still forgive;
To bear whatever comes, but still to care;
To be cheerful when you can, there's wisdom there.
Ah Prospero, I start to feel your spell;
A quiet benediction exceeds the cry from hell.

And then I reached Sonnet 51, and then I stopped.
I decided it was not time to end the old year.
It was time to begin a new one.

But my heart wandered in the desert for what seemed like the rest of the seven years.

And while wandering in the wilderness, I began to wonder about something.

Could a sonnet really be a little song if it has no melody?

Maybe every poem is really only the unfinished lyric for a song.

In the tradition of the rabbis, sacred scriptures are not merely read.

We sing them.
We sing the stories.
We even sing the laws.

I realized somehow I had to learn how to sing.

But I needed a teacher.

I found Roy.

The Prophet Elijah said:

> *I call heaven and earth to witness that whether it be Jew or Gentile, man or woman, manservant or maidservant, the holy spirit will suffuse each person in proportion to the deeds he or she performs."*

Roy and I were from different times and different places.

But I believe then when I try to sing, there is beneath the quaver of my own voice a trace . . . an echo . . . of Roy's own tones, deep and steady and true . . .

SONG 8

Roy (and a Frozen Boy from the North)

Roy
Was a child of the South
He was raised up singing
Gospel in the choir

Roy
Grew a baritone deep
Sang a baritone proud

People heard him singing, said glory aloud
People heard him singing, cried glory aloud
People heard him singing, sang glory aloud

Roy
Went out on the road
To sing for his supper
To sing for his soul

He tried to scrape a living up by singing in bars
A couple of times he warmed up for a star
Frank Sinatra heard him, said mercy on me
Sinatra himself, he cried mercy on me
Francis Sinatra sang mercy on me

But Roy
Never got off the ground
Played in too many small towns
Went too many rounds

And Roy, he started singing I just want to go home
And Roy he started crying I just need to go home
And Roy he started saying I just got to go home

Roy
Never made forty five
Didn't leave any records
Didn't leave any wife

But one last thing about Roy Legrand
Came here up North to make a final stand
Set up this school to teach people to sing
Adult beginners were his special thing

And Roy, he heard you singing, he said, "Make me believe"
Roy, he heard you singing he cried, "Make me believe"
Roy, he heard you singing he sang, "Make me believe"
I believe I believe I believe I believe I believe
I believe I believe I believe I believe I believe

And a frozen boy from the North
And a frozen boy from the North
And a frozen boy from the North
Believed that he could

And a frozen boy from the North
And a frozen boy from the North
And a frozen boy from the North
Began to believe

AFTER HE HAD his final stroke, I visited Roy in the hospital.

Roy could not talk, let alone sing,

When our eyes met, his did not seem to recognize mine.

But right there in that hospital room, I remembered a hymn that he once taught me. It was about the suffering servant of the Book of Isaiah. I sang it a cappella, and so very softly that no one outside the room could hear me.

I would like to believe he was listening.

I want to believe that he heard me.

SONG 9

Ever Faithful

The battered reed is still unbroken
The dampened wick is still alight
The suffering servant still stands waiting
Ever faithful in God's sight
The suffering servant does not lift his voice
In his silence he abides
Come ye brothers, let us sing for him
Let us sing against the tide

Ever faithful,
brothers we pray
Every faithful
all of our days
We lift up our voices to heaven

The battered reed is still unbroken
The dampened wick is still alight
Come ye brothers, let us sing for him
And may the silent dove take flight
And may the silent dove now
Fly,
Fly,
May the silent dove now fly.

My FATHER USED TO TELL ME that we should interpret our lives the way we interpreted the sacred Scriptures. Some things in the scriptures, my father said, are harsh or cruel when you first read them. And no power on earth can change the literal words on the page.

But the rabbis did not surrender.

They would find forty legal arguments to show that the passage really meant

. . . something else:
. . . something just
. . . or something compassionate.

Or the rabbis would make up a story.

Then they would pick up the words from the obstinate passage, and place them inside of that story.

And suddenly the words would appear in a warm new light.

And the cold and immutable letters of the Scriptures would find

redemption.

"Do the same with the cold hard facts of your life, my son."

And then one day I met someone . . .

SONG 10

A Touch of Courtesy

I know someone like you
Would not refuse
A touch of courtesy
A moment of your time is all I ask,
And nothing more
A little time, a little grace, a little smile, a touch of . . . empathy
Then I'll be out your doorway
I'll be out your door

I'm not asking so much
Not much more than the gentlest touch

Of a little laugh, a little joy, a little smile, a touch of . . . sympathy
That's all I ask, and then not much more
A little time, a little grace, a little smile, a touch of . . . chemistry
Then I'll be out your doorway
I'll be out your door

I've heard of too much and too soon
But I'm not asking the moon

Just a little you, a little me, and maybe for eternity,
That's all I ask, and then nothing more,
A little you, a little me, and make it for eternity
Then I'll be out your doorway
Halfway out your door

SONG II

Calm of Your Eyes

I can't recall
All the times I've been hurt before
Time after time
Many times worse than the time before
I look at you
And I do forget
What I have been through
Lost and forgotten, in the calm of your eyes
Soothed and made well, in the balm of your eyes.

A sailor who was tempest tossed
And almost lost;
pitch and yaw and roll,
Lightning flash, thunder crash, the mast is smashed
Pitch and yaw and roll,
Now becalmed upon the sea
Of tranquility
I can wait forever
For a storm to break me free

I look at you
Look at me
With such sympathy
I feel released
From the cords of old memory
I look at you

And I wonder what you have been through too
Lost and forgotten in the calm of your eyes
Soothed and made well in the balm of your eyes

ONE DAY SHE SANG a fragment of a melody. She said it was a song she had just heard on the radio. I recognized it. It was an old song, the character in it is a woman, but Roy loved it, and he used to sing it himself, and he taught it to me.

And I start to sing it with her.

SONG 12

Will You Be There?

You say I'm a flower
Splendid and new
Colours and fragrance all meant for you
The sunshine will wither the rose it will raise
Will you be there, will you be there, when the petals turn gray?

Early spring flowers
Will aim to grow high, so high, so high
Loving admirers,
Will praise to the sky, the sky, the sky
And yet when then flowers turn back to earth
There is no one to see them, and never a word

You say I'm a flower
Resplendent with dew
Flourishing sweetly and all meant for you
Will lovers sing lyrics when the bloom fades away?
Will you be there, will you be there, when the petals turn gray?

The sunshine will wither the rose it has raised
Will you be there, will you be there, at the end of the days?

When we were finished, she said "that was beautiful. Can you sing it again?"

I said "actually, that was the first time I ever sang a sound out loud for anyone."

And she said "am I just anyone?"

And I believed that we would be together. And we always have been. Even though I did not forget the sorrows I had already learned. Even though life would bring her, even apart from me, more sorrows than she had known.

And then we were married, and then our son was born. . . .

I remember . . .

It is the middle of the night. Michael, just a few months old, has woken up crying, and he has woken me up. I go to his crib and pick him up. I have never made my own song before. But I improvise the words and music, and then I go back and sing it again with a few improvements, and then I sing it again and again til it seems finished. Meanwhile, Michael is falling asleep in my arms. His cries have subsided into heavy breaths, and then his heavy breaths have become as soft and steady as a heartbeat.

SONG 13

Michael's Lullaby

Michael rest your weary head upon my shoulder
Don't you cry
Let the dark and silky milk of nighttime soothe your sleepy eyes
Not the dark of sorrow
But the usher of tomorrow
Not the dark of grief
Shelter for a tiny leaf

Michael rest your weary head beside my heart
And never fear
Let the throbbing heartbeat here inside me soothe your gentle ears
Not the dark of end
Take me with you little friend
First the night and then the dawn
Will carry you beyond beyond. . . .

Michael rest your weary head upon my shoulder and good night
Peaceful dreams and let me stay with you until the morning light

---

AND NOW MICHAEL is asleep.

But now I am awake for the rest of the night

I pull out my 51 Sonnets, and read them, until I come to this one. I read it to myself, and then I read out loud, all to myself.

Sonnet 24 / The All Creating Father

The all creating father won't reply
When scared, alone, I ask him what I'm for;
I see the ash and dust, no reason why;
The answer stays within his silent store.
I might find purpose in the task of Art
And craft a work whose truth survives the age
If I had a subtle hand and Titan's heart –
My lines will no doubt perish with their page.
So maybe I should make myself a son
A new and better world than I can be
And teach him all I can and when I'm done
I'll leave him free to find what he may seek.
But what if he returns to me once more
And scared, alone, he asks me what he's for?

For a long time after the lullabies, though, I did not even try to make up any more songs.

There were children to play with. . . .

But there were also bills to pay,

And a job to try to pay them with,

And all the scrambling and scurrying and struggling.

I felt that maybe the lullabies were all the melodies I had in me anyway.

But from time to time I could not stop myself from thinking.

I thought about generations to come and generations past.

I thought about the stories that my grandfather used to tell me too.

SONG 14

A Grandfather's Blessing

There was a time when my hands still obeyed my commands;
Back in my homeland, my grandson, I'm young as you are
My father, my mother, three brothers, two sisters together
On Friday night, Father, he blesses us at the first star

My father says "Life is a gift
A gift from above
May you grasp it and cherish it
All of your days"

A fire of hatred approaches, it burns and consumes us
All of us gone, but for me, I am pulled from the ash
I cross a sad ocean and come to the prairie to settle
It's cold and it's lonely as me as I think of the past

My father said "life is a gift . . . all of your days"
"Life is a gift all of your days"

I meet your grandmother, we marry, and we have a daughter
It's a warm day in spring when your mother is born on the farm
We struggle, it's hard, but somehow we just manage to feed her
She is safe and alive and I hold her so close in my arms

My life was a gift; a gift that I give, with all of my blessings to you
My life was a gift; a gift that I give; with all of my blessings to you

THE TALMUD SAYS that whoever kills one person, it is as if he destroys the whole world; whoever saves a life, it is as though he saves the whole world.

The rabbis meant by this that any single person may be the ancestor of a whole chain of children, grandchildren, great-grandchildren, and so on, from generation to generation.

The Torah proclaims that from generation to generation the truth must be preserved and transmitted.

The first person to learn the sacred law was Moses, on Mount Sinai.
He taught Joshua,
who in his turn instructed the next generation . . .
and so on. . . .
and so on.

The tradition holds that even now, in each of us, there is at least a tiny piece of the ancient truth.

SONG 15

A Fraction of a Tear

A humble man who bears a mighty grief
Lies down beside a river and he begins to weep
His tears are carried downward to the sea
And there they mix with other drops through all the centuries

And now
Every time you stand upon the shore
In every wave from every ocean's store
In every wave that casts a spray
Upon your face you'll feel a trace

A fraction of a tear
A fraction of a tear
A fraction of a tear of long ago

A woman held her lover's hand that day
Her touch has graced his heart as he then goes about his way
He comes upon the man who lies and weeps
Whose tears are falling downwards to the river to the sea

Stranger and my brother, are you hurt?
Let me take your arm and help you rise above this earth once more

A fraction of a tear
A fraction of a touch
A fraction of a day of long ago

And now
Every time you feel your heart will break
And every time you feel a warm embrace
Another time, another place
Is sending you another trace

A fraction of a touch
A fraction of a tear
A fraction from that day of long ago

A fraction of a tear
A fraction of a touch
A fraction of a day of long ago.

THE SCRIPTURES SAY that a man's life is a passing shadow.

The Rabbis asked: And what is it that casts the shadow?
The shadow is not cast by
a mighty wall
or a towering palm tree
or anything that seems to last a while.

It is the shadow of

a
bird
in
flight.

SONG 16

Moving Forward

Going down to a dusty basement
Used to shine here when I played
Mom is moving out tomorrow
I've come back to help her clear away

Come across a tarnished trophy
Cannot read it, what's it for?
Soccer, spelling, what's the difference?
No one else remembers anymore

I do recall a little boy who
Who used to laugh or cry
When he would win
Or he would lose a prize

Comic books stacked month by month
Report cards piled year by year
Once I knew them all by heart
Throw them out, can't stand to have them near

And finally the bicycle
That's lying on its side
My father's pushing me
It's my first ride

And he says:

"Always forward
Keep on peddling
Wheels keep turning
Moving and you're going to stay upright

Looking forward
Never backwards
I'm behind you
And I know you're going to be all right"

Twisted saddle,
Old flat tires,
I carry it upstairs
Have to go outside and get some air

"Always forward
Keep on moving
Wheels keep turning
And I know you're going to stay upright

Looking forward
Never backwards
I'm behind you
And you know you'll always be all right"

As I GREW OLDER, I began to appreciate more and more that my father had a gift.

Life is like a river, and no matter what the river, my father could make up a story about how it was for the best, and he could will himself into believing it. If the river was peaceful and blue, it was the route for navigation and refreshment for the soul. If the river froze and turned icy white, we were finally relieved of the tedium of endless summer. If the river turned turbulent and muddy, it meant that there must have been spring rain, and that was good for the crops.

I phoned him up once, in anguish. Another man stole one of my ideas and he used it to win a job that should have been mine.

My father said:

> "If you were promoted, you would only be ordering other people around.
>
> Be happy where you are.
>
> You were meant to create, not command."

I did stay, and I worked hard, and from time to time I was struck with other ideas, even bigger and better. But my best ones were never understood or appreciated.

My father said

> "If you were famous, you would have to spend more time with strangers.
> Be happy with your children instead.
> Only they will remember you."

Once I said to him, "Dad, if I stepped outside my house and was crushed by a large asteroid, you'd tell me I was lucky to have the chance to be part of a really spectacular lawn sculpture."

I used to wonder how I would get by when my father was no longer around.

I asked him once.

He said:

> "You will be better off.
>
> Without me, you will have to become stronger." So many ways to look at a river.

The Middle Ages

According to the sages, the age of forty is when you acquire understanding, and fifty is when you are ready to counsel others.

My children were not babies anymore, and sometimes I could not help thinking about how it is when you enter the middle ages.

About how you are now so

deliberate
moderate,
temperate
equable

About how you can take things

one at a time
as they came
in your stride

About how you yearn at times to find escape from the bonds of your maturity.

When I reached the middle ages, I remembered a sonnet I had written long before.

Sonnet 37 / Maturity

When my first love proved my first love in vain
I felt my heart and soul had been excised
The emptiness inside refilled with pain
And what remained unlucky it survived.
In time, by time, somehow, somewhat stored
Enough at last that I could care for you
I dreaded most that if betrayed once more
The pain would be too much to bear anew.
But when you left I stood and carried on
Woeful, weary, aching I carried on;
My new and sterner mettle can sustain
The shocks that drove the child from my frame.
And now I feel the worst I've grown too numb
To suffer as I could when I was young.

SONG 17

The Middle Ages

When you get to the middle ages,
You won't believe it's the age of faith
You're so far away from the promised home
And every road seems to lead to Rome or roam. . . .

When you get to the middle ages,
You won't know the enlightenment
All you know is you never know
You might as well accept whatever you've been sent

and sometimes
A child cries
sometimes
A child cries

When you get to the middle ages
You won't feel it's the age of romance
You are fixed like a planet in its regular track
You're not a bursting supernova that can rip up the black

But sometimes
A child smiles
Sometimes, a child smiles

It's not the age of industry
You've worked enough time in that factory,
but sometimes . . .
yeah, sometimes . . .

It's not the information age
You've been misinformed about every stage
But sometimes,
a child survives
and sometimes
a child's alive

WHEN YOU GET to the middle ages, you sometimes think wistfully about people like Winston Churchill. He is already past middle age. He has suffered many failures and frustrations. If he dies now, history will little remember him.

But suddenly, his nation is beaten on a foreign battlefield, and threatened with invasion and destruction. Churchill is called upon to lead. His principal weapon is the art of his words. He mixes plain talk and soaring eloquence; honesty and optimism; realism and resolve.

His nation rallies;

and in the end,

his nation is saved.

No matter that his people turn him out of office as soon as the war is over. Churchill and his people have already achieved their finest hour.

In the Scriptures, there are men and women who suddenly emerge from the shadows. Like Gideon in the Book of Judges.
The children of Israel have been crushed in their own land by a cruel conqueror. An angel of God summons Gideon to lead them back to freedom. Gideon replies that he is the least member of the most humble clan in his tribe. But he takes up the call.

SONG 18

Aliyah

I've lived half a life in this valley
Forgotten by people, forgotten by rain
A struggling shepherd who straggled after his lambs

I've lived half a life in this valley
A shepherd whose flock never heeded his half-hearted calling
Now all of you come down to me and ask me my plan

You must be a desperate nation
Bent down in sorrow, burdened by doubt and by sin
If now it has fallen to me to take up command

Aliyah!
Sound the horn,
Raise the torch
And I will lead you up on high

Aliyah!
Sound the horn
Raise the torch
And together we will rise

No I cannot be Moses forever,
Not even for all the days of my life
But I know that I can be Moses the length of this night

Each of us made in the image
Each of us born with an ember inside, ever waiting
Awaiting a wind that turns embers to blazoning light

Aliyah!
Sound the horn,
Raise the torch
And I will lead you up on high

Aliyah
Aliyah
Aliyah
Aliyah
And we will rise

We cannot stay righteous forever
We will slide again into old ways
And those who would be our oppressors
Will always abide

But here and now
In this time in this place
Let us resolve on this moment of grace
We are made out of clay but inside a flame's burning bright

Aliyah!
Sound the horn
Raise the torch
And I will lead you up on high
Aliyah
Aliyah
Aliyah
Aliyah yah yah yah yah yah yah

Aliyah
Aliyah
Aliyah
Aliyah yah yah yah yah

But a moment of transcendence is not always ours to have or to know or to keep.

SONG 19

Wait for a Moment

Got a songwriting man
Who can't find his muse
Looking for a melody
That he can use
So he strums all day
And he frets all night
Till the songwriting man
Is out like his light

In a dream
The melody comes
Bright and pure as a morning sun
And it seems it's been here all along
But no one else heard it
The songwriter's song

The songwriting man, he wakes up in fear
Gotta get it down while it's still in my ears

He sings
Hang on wait for a moment
Don't leave me now that you're here
Just when he reached for some paper
All the music disappeared

It's been a long time
Since that night and that morn
And the songwriting man
Is sad and forlorn
But sometimes he sings
When no one's around
And he sings about
A silent sound

He sings

Hang on
Wait for a moment
Don't leave me
Now that you're here
Just as I reached out to hold you
You just left and disappeared

AND AS THE YEARS ADVANCE, sometimes it seems as though the only thing that grows stronger within us is the intensity of our regrets.

SONG 20

Regrets (Me Oh My)

Me oh Me oh Me oh Me oh My
Me oh Me oh My
Me oh Me oh Me oh My
Me oh Me oh My

You ooh ooh ooh
Ooh ooh ooh
Ooh ooh ooh
Ooh ooh ooh

You and Me and then oh then
Me oh Me oh My
You and Me and then oh then
Me oh Me oh My

Then and now
Me and me
Then and now
You and you

Me oh Me oh Me oh My
Now and then oh My
Then and now and now and then
Me oh Me oh My

Me oh Me oh My

I ONCE SAID to my father, "You know how you're supposed to become your father when you come to be middle aged? Well you're doing a way better job of being you than I am."

He said "what do you want? You have a steady job, a nice family . . ."

I said "How about peace of mind, or creative achievement, or immortality?"

He said:

> "If you had peace of mind, you would not feel the need for creative achievement.
>
> One day you will find one or the other;
>
> As for me my son,
>
> I have never worried about being creative.
>
> I can always say that I am your father."

As each year went by, I thought more and more about the justice of this world.

When I was young, I was surprised and dismayed that life is not fair.

As I grew older, I was unsurprised and dismayed that life is not fair.

If only there were . . . someone above and beyond us . . . who would deliver us from oppression and heal the broken world . . .

SONG 21

Righteous Storm

The voice of God spoke softly to Elijah when he feared
A quiet, gentle murmuring, a still small voice, came near
The word of heaven, Scripture says, a whisper in the wind
And not in flames or earthquakes that are mightier than sin

The whisper has grown quieter
And smaller and more still
Perhaps we never heard it
And perhaps we never will

We hear instead the shouts and flames and quakes from angry men
No voice from heaven intervenes to save the innocent

Time has come for the righteous storm
Let justice sweep like a rolling thunder
Shattering idols, and humbling tyrants
Breaking the shackles, and breaking the silence

The voice of God spoke softly to Elijah when he feared,
A quiet, gentle murmuring, a still small voice, came near
The word of heaven, scripture says, a whisper in the wind
And not in flames or earthquakes that are mightier than sin

The whisper has grown quieter
And smaller and more still
Perhaps we never heard it
Perhaps we never will

FAITH, OF COURSE, is not always easy to sustain in the face of hard realities.

SONG 22

Daniel in the Lion's Den

Daniel's in the Lion's den
Daniel's in the Lion's den
Daniel's in the Lion's den
Will they be eating up the prophet?
Will they be eating up the prophet?

A bad king said
A long time ago
Daniel man, hey
You got to go
You can't go worshiping some other king
You're messing up my absolute thing

And now

Daniel's in the Lion's den
Daniels's in the Lion's den
Daniel's in the Lion's den
Is the writing on the wall?
Is the writing on the wall?

Well Daniel was a man of inedible faith
He said the Lord will protect in this terrible place
He looks a lion right in the eye
And says you won't eat me, that I prophecy

And now

Daniel's in the Lion's den
Daniel's in the Lion's den
Daniel's in the Lion's den
He can take a lot of pride
He can take a lot of pride

That's the theory, and I'm impressed
But don't volunteer me for the practical test
I could accept that ancient creed
But my problem is contemporary lions don't read about

Daniel in the Lion's den
Daniel in the Lion's den
Daniel in the Lion's den
And I'm a man who is not Dan
I'm a man who isn't Dan
That's what I am
A man who is not Dan

In the Bible itself, right from the beginning, there are two contradictory strains of thought.

One preaches that just and merciful conduct will be rewarded.

The other warns that the wicked may prosper and the righteous may perish. It is not within our powers to understand why.

The two strands of thought wrestle with each other throughout the Bible.

Earlier in the Bible, there are covenants: the people promise to be faithful to the word of the Lord, and in return he shall bring them peace and contentment.

By the end of the Jewish Bible, we find, Job, the most righteous man who ever lived, finally asking what the deal is. And God can only tell him to stop asking impertinent questions.

The Rabbis came into a world when God had fallen entirely silent but the cries of suffering were as intense as ever.

The final book of the Talmud is called Pirke Avot, the Ethics of the Fathers. In it, there is a quote from the most prominent sage of each generation of rabbis. Each sage tries to summarize his whole philosophy of life in a few words.

Rabbi Antigonus of Sokho said:

> *"We should do right without hope of reward.*

Rabbi Nittai of Arbel said:

> *We should not lose hope that there will be retribution for the wicked.*

Rabbi Yanai said:

> *"The reason why the guilty prosper or the innocent suffer is not within our grasp."*

According to legend, a rabbi finally brought a lawsuit against God for breaking his covenant to protect the children of Israel if they obeyed his Commandments.

Here is a sonnet about what happened.

Sonnet 36 / The Trial

It's said some servants of the Holy Law
Respectful of Its just and blind decrees
Believed it bound both low and high degrees;
From wounded old Jews to mighty Jeho. . . . .
Is not the breach of covenant a sin?
Did not the Lord give Abraham his word –
That Israel would be blessed by all the world
If in return it kept its faith in Him?
For breach of sacred trust their God was tried;
They offered he might speak in his defence;
And when the king of kings maintained his silence
Their wisest man was bid to plead His side.
They found Him guilty, though the trial was fair;
And then they went to say their evening prayers.

The next song begins with more ancient sayings from the Ethics of the Fathers.

A later verse is based on a Yiddish proverb that emerged after two thousand years of further experience.

The proverb is about what would happen if God lived here on this earth.

It was my own father who told me that proverb.

SONG 23

Ethics of the Fathers

The whole world
It stands
On three things:
On justice
on truth
and deeds of loving kindness

I've lived my whole life
In the company of scholars
And now I find
Nothing so becomes a man as silence

Oy, oy
If God lived on this earth
The people would throw rocks through his window

The ethics of the fathers
The wisdom of their sons
And is the cannon over?
Is the canon done?

In the book of Genesis, the world begins as chaos. But God creates order by separating things, and making them distinct. He separates light from dark, day from night, land from water. He creates animals and humankind and gives to each its own place.

Then in the book Exodus, God reveals the ten commandments. They command that each of us recognize who we are, and to be nothing else.

> Remember that you are a man, not a God;
> Honour your own father and your own mother;
> Do not covet that which belongs to another."

In the Scriptures, God tells one of his peoples, the children of Israel, that it has a particular role in history and among nations. God delivers the children of Israel out of Egypt, and reveals to them his sacred moral law. The children of Israel must obey them,and teach them to their children and by example serve as a light unto all nations.

God tells the children of Israel:

> *"I have given you this mission not because you are the greatest of nations, but rather because you are the smallest."*

The children of Israel have survived as a people because they have remembered who they are.

And the children of Israel have almost perished from the Earth for the very same reason.

It can be a terrible thing to lose your sense of your place in the world.

It can be a terrible thing to understand it.

SONG 24

Unoriginal Sin

For thirty five years now
We've worked in this store
Owe you a lot Dave but we owe the banks more
One more appliance purchased and sold
Who really cares
You know we're both getting old

I'm going down to the churchyard
Going to make the churchbells ring
Going to make the angels sing again
Going to make the churchbells ring

Sam you never even belonged to our faith
The closest you came is when you ran past our place
And we never had any choir bells
Just electrical organs that sounded like hell
Seems to me your unoriginal sin
Is trying to go back to where you've never been

Dave I can't hear what you're saying since
The customer put the appliance on rinse
Give me the dial and I'll give it a spin
Got to go back, let the cycle begin

I'm going down to the churchyard
Going to make the churchbells ring
Going to make the angels sing again
Carillons will carry on
Going to make the churchbells ring again
Pealing and appealing till the break of dawn

THE BOOK OF LEVITICUS tells the story of Azalel, the scapegoat. On the Day of Atonement, the sins of the congregation are placed upon this creature, and he is sent away all by himself, to die. The community has symbolically separated itself from its stain. But the flesh and blood scapegoat lives on, at least for a while, the most lonely and outcast being in all of creation.

SONG 25

Scapegoat

The priest proclaimed unto the congregation
That on this scapegoat we shall cast our sin
Upon him cast the sin of our whole nation
Into the desert it shall go with him

The scapegoat wanders and he finds no shelter
He stumbles and he falls and cannot rise
The burden sand reminds him of the altar
And then at last he hears a voice on high:

"Who has done this unto thee,
I shall require their cruelty,
Little goat, these prideful men
Soon shall know my punishment"

The scapegoat said, "almighty Lord
I pray you, put away your sword
A sip of water, all I seek
And nothing more do I entreat

What I want is not sacrifice, but kindness
What I want is not sacrifice, but kindness"

The scapegoat said "almighty king
They thought you wanted some such thing;

And if that is, or is not, true
I do forgive them – and you too

What I want is not sacrifice but kindness
What I want is not sacrifice but kindness"

THE SAGES TELL A STORY about the death of King Saul. The tormented first king of Israel had tried his best to serve God and his people. But he had made mistakes and lost favour with Earth and Heaven. Near the end of his days, Saul said "God is departed from me, and answereth me no more, neither by prophets, nor by dreams." But knowing his fate, Saul went to his final battle, and took with him his three sons. The sages say that he went cheerfully, knowing the measure of justice that was sure to strike him.

At least King Saul was in the end certain that what he was doing was right. But can you still go into battle if you have had a lifetime to acquire doubt as well as wisdom?

SONG 26

Ancient Warrior

I am an ancient warrior
And should I fade away?
I hear the trumpet calling
Battle on this day

There were battles when our cause was just
But the price outweighed the prize
There were battles we knew we would win
But still we lost, and still we died

We were young, and we were certain
We felt righteous, we had pride
But looking back, I hear the sighs
Of angels. . . . some on the other side. . . .

It's so easy to just step aside
And let others bear the blows
So easy to just tell yourself
What's right or wrong, who ever knows?

But now I join you brothers
Here I am
And here I stay
And here I make my stand

It's so easy to submit yourself
To time and fate's decree
Just tell yourself no child of man
Can damn the tide of history

But now I join you brothers
Here I am
And here we stay
And here we make our stand

I am an ancient warrior
I will not fade away
I hear the trumpet calling
On this judgment day

ONE TIME I said to my father, "there's a design flaw in this entire universe here. I want to relocate to a new one."

He said:

"I never expect things to be fair or people to be kind. I'm never disappointed. And occasionally, I am pleasantly surprised."

I said:

"Really? For goodness sake, Dad, you were just turfed out of your job just last month. Some junior achiever came in knowing nothing and he turfed everyone over the age of forty who did. He ripped the best people of the company. But he'll get credit for saving a few dollars in the short run, and they'll make him vice president in no time."

"So? He forced me to be a free man while I still have a few years of good health yet to enjoy it. I'll get by. My father had to work to the end of his life in a meat packing plant."

"And what about our entire people? In most places we're still not wanted, and we either flee or we are destroyed. And if we find a place we can be at home, we quietly assimilate. So what was all that suffering for? And what about our being the light unto nations?"

"And what if we do quietly disappear? Time will pass, and no one will feel the loss of something they never knew."

"Dad, you can't really believe it doesn't matter. What kind of ending would that be to the whole story?"

"Tell me, my son, has the story been a pleasant one?"

And now we are coming to the end.

The rabbis of old questioned whether we are right to celebrate birth and mourn death.

They tell a parable.

When a ship makes its maiden voyage, there is often celebration; but who knows what storms and shipwreck may befall that ship in its voyages ahead? It is when a ship arrives safely at its destination that we should celebrate. When a child is born, we celebrate, even though we do not know what the child's destiny will be; perhaps the time to celebrate is when a person has lived his life fully and leaves it peacefully and with a good name.

The rabbis could always tell a good story.

They understood the consolation of art.

SONG 27

Twilight

Sometimes
At twilight
I seem to see better
I even see someone who's no longer there

And sometimes
At twilight
The air, it seems warmer
And now I remember a childhood prayer

All of the nights that have led me to this one
I've wondered, do you wait for me?

We were two
Now I'm one
Coming home
All alone
Coming home

Since you're gone
Carried on,
All alone
Did my best
Coming home

All of the nights that have led me to this one
I've wondered, do you wait for me?

Imagine
At dayfall
There comes on a porchlight,
Imagine it's guiding me safe to your door

Imagine that porchlight
At twilight
Is your light
And we'll be together
again evermore

All of the nights that have led me to this one
I've wondered, do you wait for me?

We were two
Now I'm one
Coming home
All alone
Coming home

Since you're gone
Carried on
All alone
Need a rest
Coming home

Imagine a fireplace glowing and warming
And there you are waiting for me

All of the nights that have led me to this one
I've wondered if you wait for me

In the Jewish tradition, when a loved one passes away, you must recite the prayer called Kaddish. In the face of death, we chant in its relentless and hypnotic cadence

Yitgadal v'yitkadash sh'mei raba . . .

And the words do not lament our loss. Instead they praise God in all his power and magnificence.

Yitbarach v'yishtabach, vyitpa'ar v'yitromam . . . . .

And why at a final parting, in our desolation, we would chant in praise of the master of the Universe?

Here is a story from my father.

It takes place two thousand years ago, the time of the second destruction.

The children of Israel have revolted against their Roman masters. In return the temple is shattered and burned to the ground. Men, women and children are slaughtered. The leaders of the community, including the most learned rabbis, are hunted down.

One day a young man is forced to watch as the greatest of the rabbis is tortured to death.

This young man has been a scoffer his whole life.

In particular he used to scoff when others would say the Shehecheyanu. It is the prayer a Jew says when he reaches a blessed event in his life. It says "Thank you God for enabling me to reach this moment in time."

The young man used to laugh to himself when others said the Shehecheyanu. Yes, he would think, you have reached a happy moment; but these are far and few, and God still has in store for you much suffering and devastation.

The young man hears the dying cries of the great rabbi. The young man hears the pounding of his own heart. He hears his own short breaths. And for the first time in his life, instead of laughing to himself, the young man sings.

What he sings is the Shehecheyanu.

SONG 28

Shehecheyanu

Baruch Atah Adonai
Elohenu Melech Hoalam
Shehecheyanu
V'kiyemanu
V'higiyanu
Lazman Hazeh.

Baruch Atah Adonai
Elohenu Melech Hoalam
Shehecheyanu
V'kiyemanu
V'higiyanu
Lazman Hazeh.

AND NOW LET ME tell what happened when my father passed away.

As I was saying, for many years after I sang to my children their own lullabies, I did not make up any more songs.

I was not sure that I could.

I was not sure that I needed to.

Then later. . . .

Suddenly. . . .

I hear that my father has suddenly passed away.

I cannot even think.

But the first thing I do is sit down and I compose his eulogy.

And doing that is enough for me to carry on for a few more days, until I deliver it in the synagogue.

And then my mother asks me, what should be your father's epitaph?

I cannot even think.

But right away I say to her: "The gravestone should read:

'The wisest of minds,
The warmest of hearts,
The widest of smiles.'"

And saying that is enough for me to carry on for a few more days. And now I am back in my own town and in my own home.

When I get there, I still cannot think. But the first thing I do is I sit down at the piano. My son gathers himself next to me. He is not very little anymore, but he is not even halfway grown up either. And he is asking me if my father is in heaven.

And I hear myself singing this song.

SONG 29

Fathers and Sons

A long time ago
A long time ago
My father sang me silly Russian songs
I'd sit by his chair
Laughing along
My father seemed so strong
That I thought we'd sing till all the stars were gone

Michael,
Michael my own son,
My father's taken
My Daddy's gone

A long time ago
A long time ago
My father sang me silly Russian songs
I'd sit by his chair
Laughing along
My father seemed so strong
That I thought we'd laugh till all the stars were gone
Michael,
Michael my own son,
How do I go on,
Now that he is gone?
A long time from now

A long time time from now
Michael you might have a little son
And a long time from now
A long time from now
You can sing him silly Russian songs
Michael,
Michael my own son,
I guess that how us daddies keep on singing
On and on and on and on and on and on

AND AFTER THAT, I thought a lot again about the story my father used to tell me;
about how life is like a river;
about how life is not like a river;
and for a long time
I did not have to write any songs
but they just flowed and flowed
one after another. . . .

And now you have heard some of them. And I believe that someday there will be more.
Or at least, that's my story.

POSTLUDE: SONG 30

The River is Long

Oh, the river is wide
And I can't see to shore
And it takes us along
Till it takes us no more
I don't know the start
And I don't know the end
Maybe to darkness and silence
The river descends

I swim best I can
But try as I might,
The current is strong
My endurance is slight
Don't know the start
And I don't know the end
All I can see are some faces
And that you are my friend

Oh the river is wide
And I can't see to shore
It takes us along
Till it takes us no more
So give me your hand
And we'll float as a pair
We'll look up to the sky

We'll see birds in the air
And maybe someday we will meet
On a cloudbank somewhere

The river is long.
And the river is long

SONG 31

Temporary

A river runs
But it won't run forever
One day every river must run dry
A river runs but still a river never
Fills the sea that rests beneath the sky

And in the meantime
In between time
A river sparkles under sunlit sky

The sun may shine
But it won't shine forever
One day every sun must have its night
The sun may shine but still the sunlight never
Stops and rests a while from its flight

But in the meantime
In between time
A river sparkles under sunlit sky

Temporary you
Temporary me
Sunlight sparkle stay a while
Like sunlit rivers when they meet the sea

SOURCES

PAGE

10 "At the hour of death, a man does not jest, and so the words of a dying man are regarded as signed, sealed and delivered"; Bialik and Kavinitsky, translated by William G. Braude, Book of Legends, 583:74, quoting from the Babylonian Talmud, Tractate Bava at 175a

12 "Our days are a shadow and there is no abiding"; Cohen, Everyman's Talmud, 69, quoting from 1 Chronicles 29

14 Talmud, Tractate Eruvin 13b

17 "Forty days before the formation of a child, a Bath Kol announces, This person is to marry so-and-so's daughter"; Cohen, Everyman's Talmud, quoting from the Talmud, Tractate Sotah 2a

18 "I am the master of my fate, I am the captain of my soul"; poem *Invictus* by William Ernest Henley

21 "A friend loveth for all time, and a brother is born for adversity"; Proverbs 17:17

26 "Whoever rejoices in the suffering that come upon him in this life brings salvation to the world"; Everyman's Talmud, quoting from the Babylonian Talmud, Tractate Taanit 8a

26 "Pray that you may never suffer all that you can endure"; Kumove, Words Like Arrows, 80

26 "Are you sufferings welcome to you"; "I welcome neither the

suffering nor its rewards"; "Then take my hand and rise up"; Book of Legends 718:24,quoting from the Babylonian Talmud, Tractate Berakhot 5b

28 "I call heaven and earth to witness that whether it be Jew or Gentile, manservant or maidservant, the holy spirit will suffuse each person in proportion to the deeds that he or she performs"; Book of Legends, 354:152, quoting from Seder Eliyyahu Rabba and Seder Eliyyahu Zuta, Friedmann edition, at 48

32 "A bruised reed shall he not break, and the dimly burning wick shall he not quench; he shall make the right to go forth according to the truth"; Book of Isaiah 42:3

42 "Whoever destroys a single life is as guilty as though he had destroyed the entire world' and whoever rescues a single life earns as much merit as though he had rescued the entire world"; Talmud, Sanhedrin 37a

42 "The first person to learn the sacred law was Moses, on Mount Sinai. He taught Joshua, who in turn instructed the next generation . . ."; Kravitz and Olitsky, Pirke Avot (Ethics of the Fathers) 1:11

44 Book of Legends, 589:44, quoting from Rabbi Huna in the Babylonian Talmud

48 "According to the sages, the age of forty is when you acquire understanding, and fifty is when you are ready to counsel others"; paraphrase of Everyman's Talmud, 73, quoting from Pirke Avot 5:21.

60 "And, behold, the LORD passed by, and a great and strong wind rent the mountains, and broke in pieces the rocks before the LORD; but the LORD was not in the wind: and after the wind an earthquake; but the LORD was not in the earthquake. And after the earthquake a fire; but the LORD was not in the fire: and after the fire a still small voice"; 1 Kings 19

64 "We should do right without hope of reward"; Pirke Avot, 1:3

64 "We should not lose hope that there will be retribution for the wicked"; Pirket Avot 1:8

64 "The reason why the guilty prosper or the innocent suffer is not within our grasp"; Pirket Avot 4:15

66 "Simon the Righteous was one of the Great Assembly. His motto was "The world standings on three things - the Torah, the [Temple] service, and loving acts of kindness; Pirke Avot, 1:2. Rabbi Shimon, the son of Gamliel, said, "The world stands on three things: on truth, on judgment, and on peace." Pirke Avot 1:18"

66 "I've lived my whole life in the company of scholars, and now I find nothing so becomes a man as slience" Pirke Avot 1:17

66 "If God lived on this earth people would throw rocks through his windows"; Words Like Arrows, 107

71 "God is departed from me, and answereth me no more, neither by prophets, nor by dreams"; Book of Legends, 116:77, quoting from 1 Samuel 28:15

74 "When a ship makes its maiden voyage, there is often celebration; but who knows what storms and shipwreck may befall that ship in its voyages ahead? . . . perhaps the time to celebrate is when a person has lived his life fully and leaves it peacefully and with a good name." Paraphrase of Everyman's Talmud, 75–76. which is quoting from Ecclesiastes Rabbah